BREAK DANCING

ANCING

CURTIS MARLOW

A STARBOOK • SHARON PUBLICATIONS • CRESSKILL, N.J. 07626

Editor: Mary J Edrei
Cover and Book Design: Rod Gonzalez
Research Assistant: Nancy Hite

Special thanks to Cathy Yelverton, Russell Simmons, Monica Lynch, Sharon Lee, Cynthia
Horner and Nike sportswear for their invaluable help. (Make-up and hair by Debra Reece).

Photo credits: Dick Zimmerman, Orion Pictures, John Cavanaugh and gratitude to Gary
Azon staff photographer for his great cover, inside color and major contributions to this book.

CHAPTER

The History of Break Dancing

there is a little-known culture that has risen up from the South Bronx and started to make its mark on the American way of life. These street-wise youngsters have their own language, music, art and dance. They seem to exist within their own self-imposed parameters. It is an insulated culture that remains pure and unyielding, in a society that manipulates taste and opinion. These young kids are able to withstand the pressures of parents, peers and media. Their aesthetic values are clearly unique. They are called B-Boys and B-Girls, and it is known as the Hip-Hop culture. Their numbers have grown since they first surfaced in the Bronx. Now B-Boys can be found in Chicago, Detroit, New Orleans, Washington D.C., Los Angeles and Memphis.

America was first exposed to the culture through the youngsters' art. We called it graffiti at first, but some of the art won the respect of conventional artists. America got a closer look at these kids through the B-Boys music. Many thought that it was just a passing fad, but RAP music is still with us. B-Boys dance, my goodness do they dance! They move like no one else. And now, America is fascinated with the B-Boy's dance. America and the World want to learn this incredible dance. America and the World wants to "BREAK."

Breakdancing, with its head spins and shoulder stands allowing only the support from the arms, which are strategically placed on the ground, is sweeping the nation. To some it may even look dangerous as these dancers demonstrate their skill. It is a visually dazzling skill.

Sally Somer, in the December 1983 issue of *In Performance*, a monthly guide to the Brooklyn Academy of Music, described breakers as, ". . . twirling around the axes of their upper bodies like human coffee-grinders, using fast pedaling footwork twisting belly-up, belly-down, finishing with elaborate leg pretzels . . ." These dancers are able to make the human body, made of bone and muscle, look like a piece of melted cheese. The flexibility they display is enough to make any professional dancer jealous. No part of the body escapes the imagination of this "street wise" dancer. The pinky finger and stomach can even play a part in this new popular art form.

But where did this dancing style come from? The streets of the South Bronx, Harlem, East Harlem, or the lower East Side of New York? Maybe Atlanta, Ga., Chicago, Ill., or Los Angeles, Ca.? Would it startle you to discover that three neighboring countries in West Africa: Mali, Gambia and Senegal provide the "roots" for this new sensation. " . . . these dancers ("Breakers") are more than just entertaining anecdotes, the performers and dancers are living links in an ancient dance tradition whose roots run deep into Afro-American cultures, whose values are like those of an older and vigorous African Heritage"—Sally Sommer.

Imagine "breaking" to the beat of African drums. That is what the young dancers of the Repertory Dance Company of East Harlem, New York, do when they perform "Ibedi-Bedi." The dance was originally choreographed by Chuck Davis, founder of the Chuck Davis Dance Company, a well-respected American-African Dance troupe. This dance was later revised by Al Smith and Cathy Yelverton, two alumni of this famous choreographer. "Ibedi-Bedi" is a dance that is done when one warrior passed on, the young men must show strength and unity to take their place as future leaders. This dance offers an excellent opportunity to see how modern "breakdancing" connects with the highly acrobatic social dancing of West Africa.

Cathy Yelverton is presently a dance teacher in the New York City School System and the guiding force behind the Repertory Dance Company of East Harlem. She is a lecturer who has taught West African Dance and Folk Lore at Hunter College in New York. Four years ago, Cathy had the opportunity to see first hand the amazing resemblance between our "breaking" and the dance done by the West Africans. "Although all the people of the region do this highly exciting social dance, it is the Fula that most resembles our kids," Yelverton says. Cathy, who has danced professionally and appeared on the Richard Pryor TV specials,

Cathy Yelverton

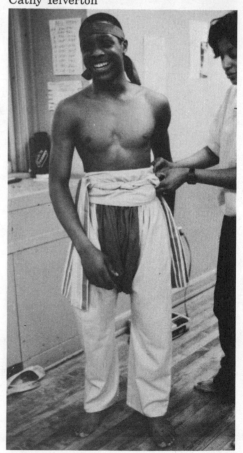

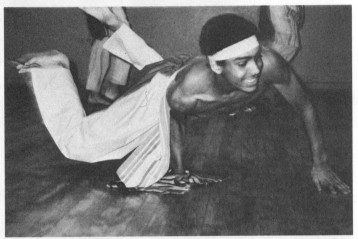

11 BREAKDANCING

Afrika Bambaataa

recalls the astonishment that showed in the faces of the African dancers, and later laughter, when she told them that young people were doing this in America. "Only men do this style of dancing, so it is not like here, where everybody breaks," she says. "They kept laughing at me. The reason they laughed was because the men who do it there range in age from young adulthood to about 50-years-old."

Not just the moves, but the attitude is the same. "They do the head spins, shoulder moves—all of it," Cathy assures. "I even noticed that they would end a difficult movement the same way our kids do, with a nonchalant freeze, she says. Not only are the physical movements shared, but the spiritual feeling of togetherness is also part of "breaking." Like Afrika Bambaataa, of Soul Sonic Force, once said, 'Instead of fighting why not have a contest to see who is the best dancer?' Well that's what they do in Africa, they don't fight, but they dance to see who is the best."

The camaraderie that develops between members of the "crews" (breaking groups) can be felt as you witness their performance. The support and respect they offer one another is commendable. Even as the "crews" compete there is mutual respect for the talent and hard work that each group displays. It is heartwarming to see the way in which the older members of the group teach the young kids, who are trying to learn.

How did this African social dance find its way to America? How did it develop into "breakdancing?" Actually, it went the course of a "quickie evolution" that took about 16 years. It seems that in the late 1960s, close to '68, many professional West African dancers came to America and settled in the Bronx, especially the South Bronx. In fact, Chuck Davis, who now has two companies—one in N.Y. and another in Durham, North Carolina, started in the Bronx. Davis is credited with starting the Brooklyn Academy of Music's Dance Africa Series. Many of these dancers, who had settled in the Bronx danced with such companies as the Senegalese Ballet in Africa. Dancers like Irabim Camara and Drummers like Ladji Camara, who are legendary, were in the public schools as teachers-in-residence. They offered master dance classes to the professional American Companies like the Chuck Davis Dance Company and the International African Ballet.

Many of the American Companies also went to Africa to study. They brought back with them an enormous amount of African culture. The knowledge that these dance companies gained was used in performances at public schools, dance mobiles, museums, community centers, etc. In fact, these groups saturated the South Bronx with African Dance, and sitting in the audience were the breakers of today, soaking it all up. For some it was no surprise, in 1971, when a group of kids in the Bronx started to do a strange new dance and lived for the "Beat."

"Mixing dance with everyday life, they used improvisation, magic circles, "call and response" patters, competition, acrobatics, undulation, sides, and complicated body and foot rhythms, demonstrating that these dancers and dances are merely the most recent blooms on the ancient black tree"—Sally Sommer.

So, breakdancing encompasses two continents and several cultures. It was sparked by an African-American cultural exchange that caused a rapid evolution in American social dance. It started with a small group of youths in the Bronx and now it has spread all over the world. The international interest in breakdance is incredible. People all around the world are amazed by this wonderful new dance. Everyone that is, except a group of Africans who have been doing the dance for hundreds of years.

HISTORY

Where does the term "breakdance" come from? In the 1970s, the world "break" took on a new meaning for a large portion of the urban community. Inner city kids started to refer to outbursts of anger as breaking. For example, "the bank would not cash her check, so she just started breaking on them." This means that she got loud and caused a scene. When someone was "breaking" back then, people didn't gather around to watch. They quickly tried to get out of the way. Another term that was used at the time, with the same meaning, was "go-off." People would get upset in a certain situation and "go-off" or "break." These terms were later used to describe wild dancers. At a party or a dance there was always someone who couldn't dance well, but made up for it with enthusiasm. This dancer would wave his hands fanatically and move all over the floor in a shaking motion. Most people would laugh at him and say that he was just going-off, or breaking.

Around the time that a song by James Brown, "On The Good Foot," came out, youngsters started doing some fancy foot-work. People would gather around these hot dancers and root them on. These kids were breaking and getting off. The term Breaking later evolved into the title of the dance done by the B-Boys.

Today, the word "Breaking" is greatly misused. People label all the dances that the B-Boys do as breaking. They tend to label all street dancing as breakdance. That is simply incorrect. "Breakdance" is the specific moves that are done on the floor, such as the spins, the wind mills, the 1990s, the swipes, and the footwork. The only standing moves that the breaker does is top-rocking and up-rocking.

The dance that is most often confused with breaking is the Electric Boogie. The Electric Boogie is all the mime-like movement that you see the kids doing. The moon-walk, waves, popping, and the robot are all moves of the Electric Boogie. As a rule, the youngsters don't do both dances. Most crews (groups of dancers) have members who just boogie and members who break. It is seldom that a dancer does both, and if he does, he is not really respected as being good at either. Clearly, Boogie is Boogie and Breaking is Breaking, and never the twane shall meet.

The history of Electric Boogie is a little easier to trace. Its origins are clearly visible. Two young entertainers were singularly responsible for black youths interest in mime, and the development of the electric boogie. Their names are Robert Shields and Lorene Yarnell. During the summer of 1977, the comic mimes "Shields and Yarnell," had a mini replacement television series on CBS. The six-week long comedy variety series got such good ratings that the network decided to add the show to their fall line-up. Shields, who had studied with Marcel Marceau, had developed his own style of comic mime, and it could be seen weekly on television. Robert and Lorene brought to life a robot couple named the Clinkers. The young black kids were all talking about the robot characters. Shields and Yarnell instantly won the youngsters' respect. And, as with most things that fascinate young people, they started to imitate. But, soon the imitators were getting really good! Shields had studied mime for years in Paris and here in the

States. But these youths were just watching television, and in a matter of weeks becoming proficient in an area that professionals study for years. At first the kids copied Shields and Yarnell to the letter. But, soon urban black youngsters started to tell their own stories through the mime that they had learned. They took it to the streets instantly. The robot dance started to show up at dance clubs all over the country. The urban youth had found a new way of communicating.

The kids are still in the streets telling their stories to anyone that will listen. They gather on street corners along with breakers and put on mini shows for nickels and dimes. You can tell from the looks on their faces that it's not just the money. These kids love communicating something that is inside of them. That's entertainment.

You will find these kids on the streets of the larger urban areas. They are now and then asked to move along by the police, but that doesn't stop them from finding a place to perform. Shields, who used to do his mime on the streets of San Francisco, used to run into the same kind of problem. His act caused him to be arrested four times. "Performing without a permit" was the charge that first time, in 1971. However, Shields just kept on taking his art to the people. It was that kind of determination that finally won him his television show. No one knew where it would ultimately lead them, but you can see that same determination on the faces of today's young street dancers.

BREAKDANCING 16

CHAPTER

Warm Up And Safety

Breakdancing is more of an athletic workout than it is a dance, in most respects. It is strenuous and requires a great deal of agility. Therefore, your approach to breakdancing must be similar to that of a sport. Most serious breakdancers are in better shape than many professional athletes. The breaker must be in good physical condition and there are a few precautions that must be considered.

If your gym activity in school has been restricted or limited by a doctor or school nurse, you shouldn't attempt breakdancing without permission. If you suffer from dizziness or shortness of breath, you should check with a physician before attempting to break. If you have any health problems, play it safe and don't start until your doctor has given you the OK.

For breaking and boogie, you are going to need a large cleared area. It is important that your space is free from objects hanging and on the floor. Coming in contact with pieces of furniture while breaking, can be dangerous as well as destructive. The best surface is a smooth wood or tile floor. The ideal surface would be a freshly polished wooden gymnasium floor. The area should be swept clean and then checked for nails, broken glass, or any other objects that may be lodged in the surface.

There will be a temptation to outfit yourself in some flashy dancing gear. Forget that for now. There will be plenty of time for putting together a costume. In the beginning, the main concern in dressing is protection! As a breaker you will need to have most

Exercise model: Paul Selik

of your body covered. Your arms, back and head are best protected with a pull-over hooded sweatshirt. A good pair of loose fitting jeans are the best protection for below the waist. These layers of clothing will help protect you from some of the bumps, bruises, scrapes, and abrasions headed your way.

Sneakers are just about the only safe footwear for breakers. They offer excellent support and the soft material cushions the foot. Sneakers should fit snugly, but not tight. High top sneakers offer the most support, but some breakers complain that they are restrictive. It seems that the high back makes certain moves impossible. You may feel that the support is more important. A thick pair of sweat socks should be worn under the sneakers. The sneaker laces are tied loosely, but we'll explain that later.

WARM UP

Your warm up will probably be one of the most important safety measures that you can take. It prepares your body for conditions that it is not used to—increased heart beat and extraordinary muscle activity, just to name two. Warm up is a necessary part of breakdance and electric boogie. Warm up must proceed every breakdance session. Most people find warm up exercises relaxing.

For breaking, we start our warm up with a series of stretching exercises. Standing straight, with hands on hips, slowly lean to the left. Don't try to lean too far, just a little at first. Then, slowly lean to the right side. Remember not to lean too far. Repeat the motion from left to right until it becomes smooth and effortless. Next, you bend forward very slowly. Lean as far as you can without straining. Then, hold this position for a few seconds, and slowly stand straight again. Push ups are a good warm up for the arms, but don't do more than five. Remember, we don't want to tire the muscles before we start. For the legs we do deep knee bends. They are done slowly, and again, no more than five.

❶

The next exercise is done on the floor. You sit with your legs as far apart as possible, without straining. Starting with your back straight and your hands on your hips, you slowly lean forward, while sliding both hands along your legs. Bend as far as you can without straining, making sure that you slide smoothly towards your ankles. Don't try to overdo it. Some of you will only be able to get past your knees, but that is okay. The more you practice the more loose you will become. Once you are leaning as far forward as you can, hold it there for a few seconds then slowly lean back to a straight sitting position. Slow jumping jacks are a really good way to get the heart going. Also, try touching your toes, but stay down for a few seconds.

One of the most important exercises is a relaxation technique. You start by finding a quiet spot where you won't be bothered. It helps if you play some soft music while doing the exercise. You start by removing your shoes and lying flat on your back. Place both hands at your sides. Try to relax. Keep shifting until you find the most comfortable position. Now, take a deep breath and slowly blow it out.

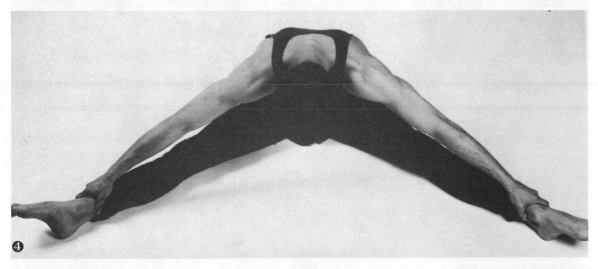

①

②

③

BREAKDANCING 26

This is a simple leaning exercise. You start from a standing position. Grasping your upper thighs, you lean backwards as far as you can without straining your back. Make certain that you move very slowly. Keep doing the exercise and each time you will be able to go back further and further. When your head is facing behind you, remove your hands from your thighs and lower them beneath you. Try to touch one hand on the floor. You may fall a couple of times, but get up and try it again. Soon you will be able to touch both hands with ease. In a few weeks you'll be able to rest your palms on the floor and lift up on your toes, forming a graceful arch with the body. This arch stretches almost every muscle in the body.

This is another back stretching exercise, but this one starts from a kneeling position. Tuck your legs behind you and rest your buttocks on your heels. You simply lean back onto the floor, stretching your arms out behind you. Reach and arch your back and the exercise is complete.

Listen to the music and try to leave your mind blank. You are going to relax your entire body one part at a time. Keeping your eyes closed, concentrate on your fingertips. Try to feel them from the tip to the first joint. Feel the nails and the other side. Next, you simply tell them to relax! Then, move on the next joint of the fingers and repeat the process. You continue through each joint, then the palm and forearm. You keep going up to the elbow and shoulders. You will be relaxing each section of the body as you go. Once you've reached the shoulders, head down the chest, back and stomach, giving individual attention to each area. You keep going until you've reached the tips of your toes. This is an extremely beneficial exercise for those who want to become good at the electric boogie. The exercise puts you in contact with your body. You develop a new relationship with your hand. You will recognize the hand as a network of bones, joints and muscles. You'll soon be able to relate to each of the body's parts. For electric boogie, the bonus is better control of movement. You will notice the difference in no time.

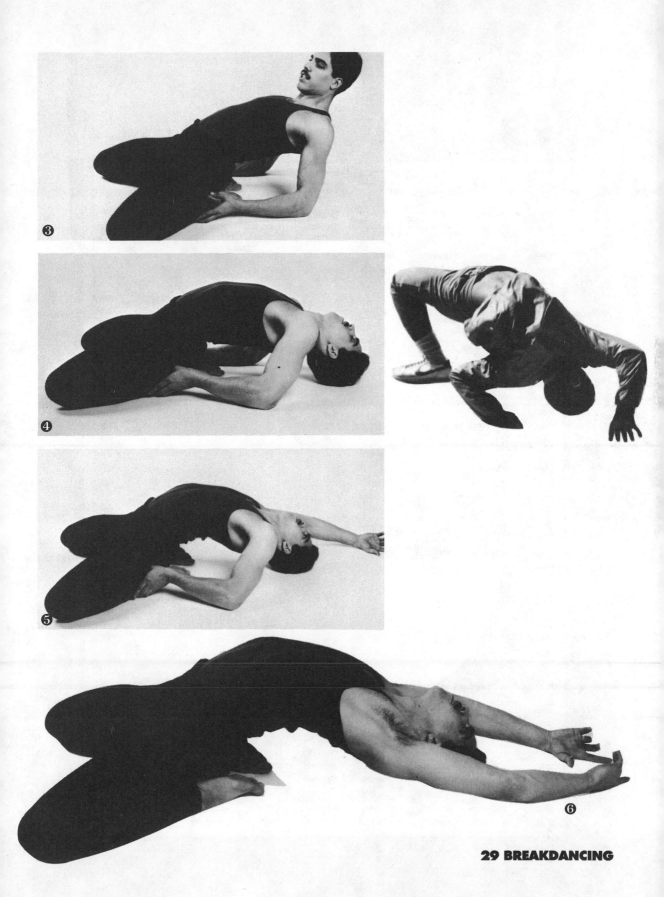

③

④

⑤

⑥

CHAPTER

Break Instructions

All breakdancing starts with top-rocking. It is somewhat of a traditional ceremony. It prepares the breaker for the incredible task ahead of hirn. It looks a lot like the shadow-boxing that a fighter does. You move your feet back and forth to the music, in an almost shuffling motion. The hands strike out much like karate moves. Just let your hands and feet move with the music. Your hands can make circle motions around the head. Cross the arms in front of you. Swing the arms behind you. Rock them out like you are boxing. Let your arms hang towards the floor. Swing your arm as if it held a saber. You can mix all these moves together, as long as you keep it in time with the music. You have also got to keep the feet moving from side to side or front to back. Bend your knees, and just feel the music as you're dancing, and you are top-rocking.

TOP-ROCKING

33 BREAKDANCING

❶ ❷ ❸ ❹ ❺

35 BREAKDANCING

UP-ROCKING

Up-rocking is a lot like top-rocking, but there is a subtle difference. To up-rock you have to move the feet a bit more. This is the move that will take you down to the floor. So, cross the legs. Bend the knees and go down to touch the floor and pop back up. Remember, music is important. You've got to stick to the beat. Shuffle, skip, and hop to the beat. Try to make the foot moves as funky as possible. This is the prelude to the foot-work.

◼ FOOT-WORK

Now you are going down to the floor. You can get down to the floor simply by bending your knees and leaning back to the floor. You come to rest on the palm of your hand. From that position you are ready to go straight into your foot-work. Using at least one hand to support you, scramble around the floor in a circular motion. With your knees bent, you take little scooting steps that propel you around the floor. At first they will be awkward moves, but after some practice your foot-work will become clean. You soon will be twirling your feet under you, but always to the beat.

37 BREAKDANCING

SWIPES

Swipes are best done from the foot-work position. All you have to do is pick up some speed in your foot-work until you've got some momentum going. Then you plant both hands on the floor and shift the momentum to your waist. By twisting your waist and lifting your legs for a moment, you'll be taking a swipe. The weight will be on your hand, and your legs will be in the air making a quick swiping turn. Then, return to the floor for more footwork. At first the swipes will be low. After some practice your swipes will get higher in the air. They may be wide, vicious swipes, but always to the beat.

BREAKDANCING 38

KNEE SPINS

Knee spins will come out of your foot-work also. It looks really simple, but it takes a great deal of balance and coordination. The body weight is rested on one knee, while the other leg is extended back. The trunk of the body is leaned forward, parallel to the floor. The hands are used only to propel the body into a spin on the knee. It may be difficult to balance at first, but don't be afraid to use both hands to steady yourself while trying to spin. After a few spills and some steady practice, your knee spins will be on the money.

HAND GLIDE

This move is nothing more than spinning your body on one hand. You must first learn to balance your body weight on one hand. That is best accomplished by practicing balancing yourself on both hands. You start by laying face down on the floor. With your upper-arms to your sides and your elbows bent, lift your body weight onto your palms. At first you may have trouble staying up, but in time you will be able to keep your feet and trunk afloat. The next step is to try to keep yourself up on one hand. This should not take you too much time. After you feel secure on one hand, find a cloth to use as a cushion under your hand. This cloth will make it easier for you to spin. Some breakers simply pull their jacket sleeves down and use them as a cushion. Once you have got yourself in the air on one hand, you use the other to propel your body around. Now, you are Hand-Gliding.

WINDMILLS

Whether you start from foot-work or up-rocking, the windmill begins from the same position. Place your hands in front of you on the floor. You will be in the position used for push-ups, but the legs will be spread apart at about a 45 degree angle. Balancing your weight between your hands and your toes, allow one of your arms to collapse. You roll over onto that same shoulder as you push off with the other hand. At the same time you swirl your legs up in the air, keeping them in that 45 degree angle. This will send you rolling on your shoulders, back and head. This will return you to almost the same position. Repeat the entire move again and again until you get enough momentum going to keep spinning with your legs in the air. Your arms are now folded over your chest. Centrifugal force will keep you rolling on your shoulders, back and head. At first you'll just rock a few times, but with practice you will learn to shift your weight to keep you going for as long as you want. Remember, this move is bound to bring you some bumps and bruises, and maybe some black and blue marks, but most breakers say that the dazzling display of a good windmill is well worth it.

BACK-SPIN

There are a countless number of ways to approach the back spin. Because it is so popular, kids have been trying it on their own and inventing new ways of doing it. The best way to learn the move is not the easiest. To make the back-spin look smooth and effortless it must be done the right way. You should start from the same position that you started the windmill with. Again, place your hands in front of you on the floor. You will be in the position used for push-ups, but the legs will be spread apart at about a 45 degree angle. Balancing your weight between your hands and your toes, you allow one of your arms to collapse. You roll over onto the same shoulder as you push off with the other hand. At the same time you swirl your legs up in the air, but this time you swirl them in a circular motion. This time the legs are whipped straight up in the air and you will be sent spinning on your back. At first you may only spin a half turn, but that is the way you learn. Keep it up, and soon you will be spinning like a top.

❶ ❷

1990

This is a very acrobatic move. It requires a great deal of balance. You are going to have to learn to stand on your hands. The secret of that is to use your legs as counter balances, thus keeping you from falling over. You go into this move from up-rocking. You begin by flipping yourself down onto one hand, then the other, for a hand stand. You then quickly shift your weight from one hand to the other, causing you to turn 180 degrees. You then flip yourself back onto your feet, and continue up-rocking. The move is done very quickly, but you will have to start very slow. After some steady practice you will be able to flip down onto your hands, turn around, and pop back up on your feet in one quick smooth move.

BREAKDANCING 46

③

④

47 BREAKDANCING

ELBOW SPIN

This spin is approached in the same manner as the 1990. You are going to have to balance yourself on your hand again. This time, when you get balanced you will do a different move. Using your other hand to maintain balance, you lower yourself onto your elbow. This is easier said than done. You will tumble over many times before you get it right. Once you've gotten the body weight on the elbow, you are going to spin, using the free hand to propel you. Remember, this is an advanced move and will take time to perfect. Don't give up, when done right the move is fresh!

HEAD SPINS

The hardest part of this move is learning to balance your weight on your head. Of course you will begin by using your hands to steady yourself. You must also move your legs in different positions, using them as counter-balances. Once you can balance yourself on your head, you will use your hands to propel you around. At first you will not be able to make a full turn, however with some practice you will find yourself spinning longer and longer. You may want to use some kind of cloth or pad as a cushion between the floor and your head. It looks hard, but keep with it, and your head spins will have everyone going in circles.

FREEZE

This move is exactly what it sounds like. After a series of serious footwork, or outrageous swipes you will want to end it with a dead "Freeze." All you do is stop all motion with a nonchalant pose. You hold that pose for a few seconds, as if you were waiting for photographers to take your picture. You can make up your own Freeze, but here are a few hot ones for you to start with.

COMBINATION BRIDGE TRACK

51 BREAKDANCING

CHAPTER

Electric Boogie Instructions

Learning to do the electric boogie can only start with waves. Waves are the fluid body movement made by the dancers. It starts at one point and literally moves like a wave through the hands, arms, shoulders, and the rest of the body. You start by extending the right arm. Close your eyes and imagine a wave coming into your hand and travelling across your arm, but don't move your arm. Just try to feel the sensation of it moving slowly across your arm. Become familiar with the feel of the imaginary wave. Now, you can open your eyes and move to a mirror. Extend your right arm out to the side, with your fingertips pointing upward. Watching your hand in the mirror, let the wave enter your fingertips. Keeping the rest of your body (especially the hand) completely still, allow the wave to bend just your fingertips downward. As the first joints bend as far as they can, allow the wave to enter the second joint and follow the first one, in a smooth downward motion. Allow the wave to move slowly from joint to joint and into the palm. As the wave leaves the bottom of the palm and travels through the wrist, three things happen simultaneously. The hand turns slowly counter clockwise, which raises the forearm, and the fingers arch upward to pick-up another series of waves. The wave then moves into the upper arm and it is lifted slightly. Allow the wave to enter your shoulder and lift it. You have completed your first wave. Keep doing it over and over again and watch it closely in the mirror. It will look awkward at first, but keep on waving. The move will become smoother in

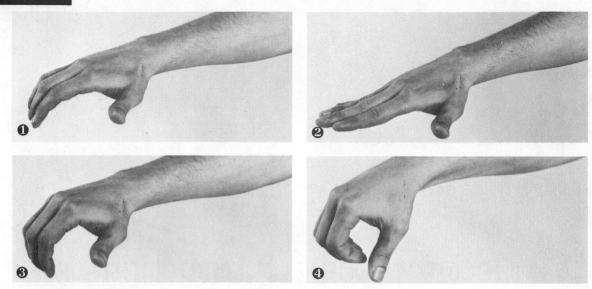

time. The more practice the better your waves will become.

Soon, the waves will be refined and they will become second nature. You will start to do them faster and more fluid. Now you are ready to move the wave across to your other shoulder. Allow the wave to move across your neck, forcing your head to move in a small circular motion, which will send the wave into the right shoulder. The shoulder is arched and passes the wave onto the upper arm, and so on. It is simply the reverse of the pattern that you have just learned. Keep practicing and the waves will move from fingertips to fingertips with ease. After you have mastered the wave from your right hand across to your left hand, try the reverse and send the wave back in the other direction. The move will become comfortable shortly and you will be able to wave in time with music. By this point you will have developed a totally new relationship with your body that will make learning the rest of the waves easy. Instead of sending the wave from shoulder to shoulder, you allow the wave to enter the upper chest. This will push the chest forward slightly. As you allow the wave to descend into the abdomen, the chest is pulled back and the stomach starts to push out. The wave pattern continues down through the pelvis, thighs, legs, and feet. Practice in front of a mirror. Remember, it is going to look clumsy at first, but don't let that stop you. Just by practicing, you can make the moves as smooth as silk.

If more than one of you are learning to wave at the same time, you may want to try a chain. This is when one dancer sends a wave to another, forming one large chain wave. It is passed from fingers to fingers.

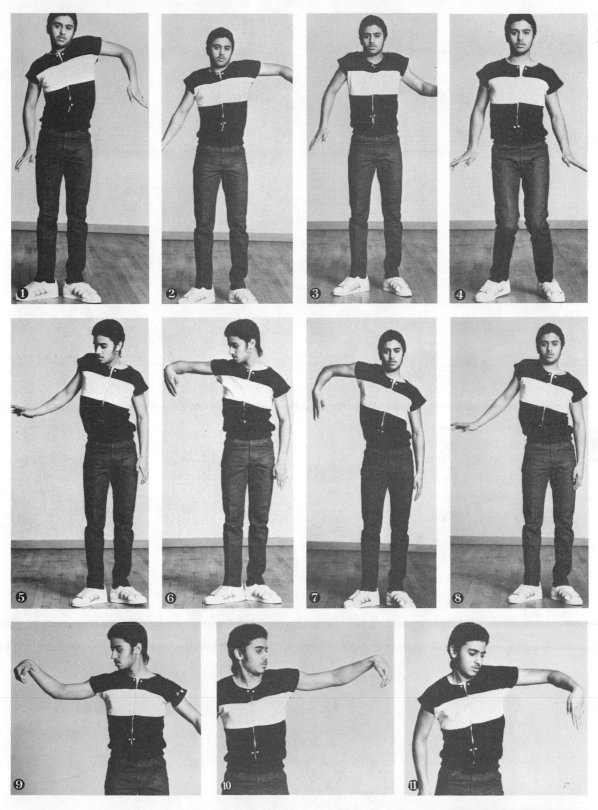

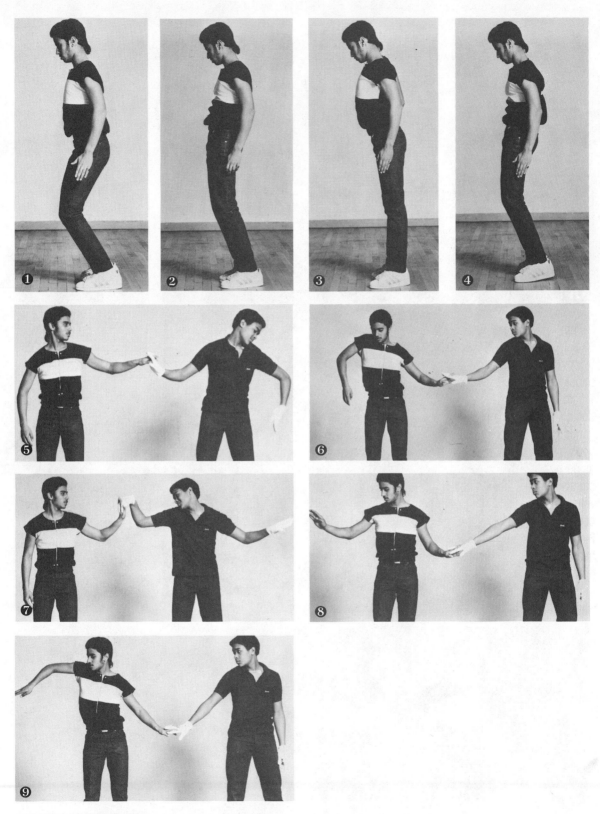

POPPING

Popping really isn't all that different from waves. Your approach is really the same, in that the motion is still from joint to joint. However, we are not talking about smooth waves, but rough jerks; popping. You can start by jerking the joints of your fingers inward towards the palm. Then pop the wrists downward. You should try doing this to music right from the start. Also, try to pop both hands at the same time. After you feel comfortable with the hand pops, then move to the right hand only. Jerk the joints of the hand as described. Think of each jerk as being a heavy jolting electrical shock. Pop these joints as if they were each getting 1,000 volts of the power company's hottest juice. When you pop the elbow, the forearm goes up. Shock the shoulder and it pops up. From the right shoulder volts travel into the neck and pops the head to the left side and jerks the left shoulder up. The jolts pop right out of the left hand. This should be done to some really jumping music. Watch yourself in the mirror as you practice. Soon you will find yourself improvising and popping in your own individual style. You will know when you are ready to pop your chest, stomach, hips, knees, and ankles. You may want to try something that a lot of poppers are doing. They kind of freeze with their knees pointed in and their elbows pointing out to the sides. They look like they are just hanging there on a hook or something. Then you can pound your elbow or knee with a closed fist and send another series of pops through the body. Keep practicing with music and your entire body will become a popping machine. You will give up control of your body to the music. It will all become automatic and the music will pop your joints effortlessly to the beat. Pop on!

59 BREAKDANCING

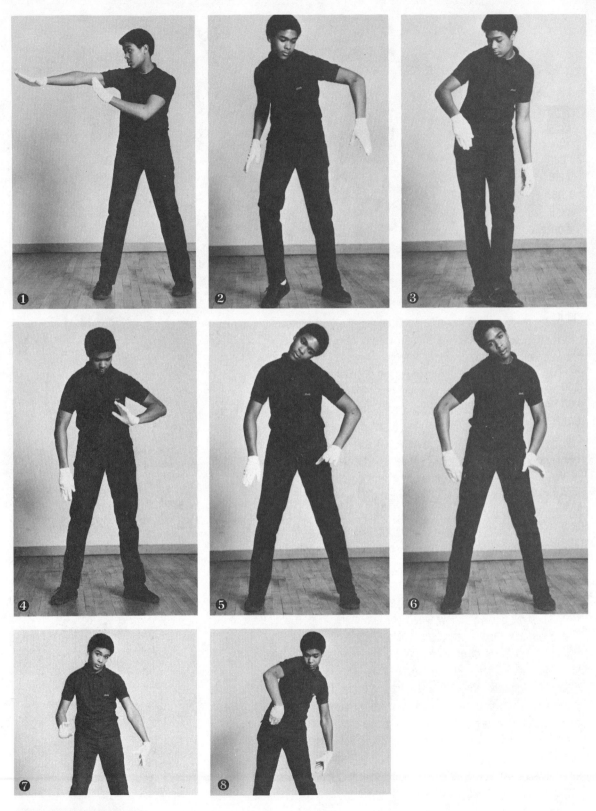

BREAKDANCING 60

THE ROBOT

Now, while you are communicating so well with your body, is the perfect time to learn the robot. Let's start with the head. What you are going to do is limit the mobility of the head. Imagine that the head has only one moveable junction, at the base of the neck. In your mind replace that flexible joint with a flat steel gear, that only allows you to move your head from left to right and right to left. Try moving your head from side to side in short measured movements. In the mirror it should look like the movement of a bird's head. Keep a blank expression on your face. Don't allow your eyes to fix on anything. Keep practicing in front of a mirror and it will start to look more and more like a robot. Now, look at your hand. You are going to limit its movement. The fingers will only move in unison. They have gears at the knuckles that join the fingers to the palm and the fingers can bend there. Hold your hand straight and try to bend the fingers forward with a series of short jerking motions, while the rest of the hand and arm are held completely still. Again, keep practicing in front of the mirror and your robot will get better. Now find the next joint on the fingers. They too have gears and can bend forward. After you have bent the bottom joints of the fingers, try bending the fingers at the joints above, in the same slow jerking motion.

Make certain not to bend the end joints of the fingers. Repeat the series. First bend the lower gears, then the upper gears. The more you practice the more mechanical the motion will become. It shouldn't take you long to become comfortable with this move. Next, try moving the head and the hand at the same time, in unison. This will be easy. You will see yourself becoming better each time you do it. Now you can move to the wrist. It, too, has a gear that allows it to bend forward. By now you have an idea of how to move it mechanically. Practice moving the wrist then move on to the elbow. Remember, the elbow has a gear that allows the forearm to move up and down, while the upper arm remains perfectly still. That is the secret of the robot, to make every part of the body move independently as if it were being operated by a gear. The upper arm follows the same pattern. There is no difference with the legs and the waist. Once you have made the adjustment in your mind, your body will become a network of gears, and will respond mechanically to music.

❶

THE ROBOT

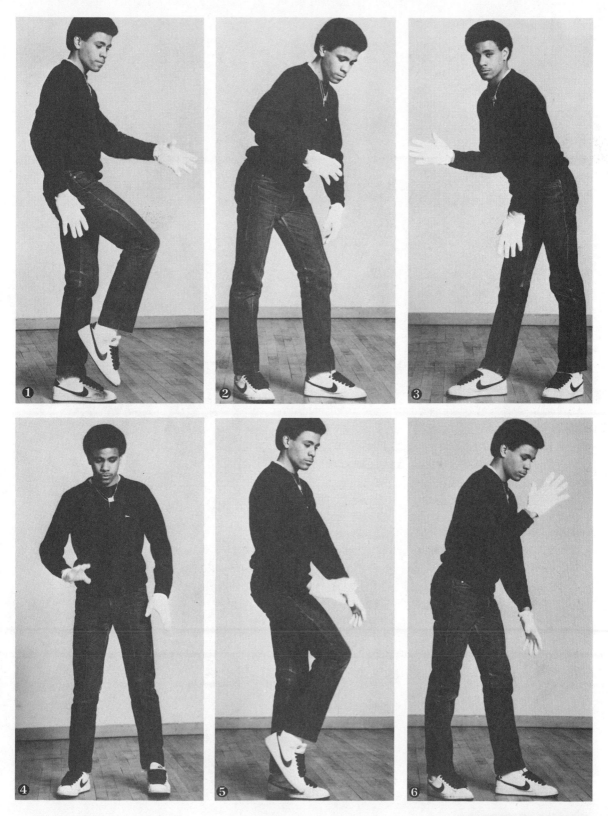

MOON WALK

We have saved the best for last. The moon walk is by far the most dazzling display of body control. Nothing captivates an audience more than seeing a boogier gliding backwards across the floor. It really isn't that hard to learn. It just takes a lot of concentration and practice.

NOTE: You are going to need some sneakers that offer you excellent support. They have to be the correct size also. You can't squeeze into tight tennis shoes and expect to do the moon walk!

The secret to doing the moon walk is very simple. You have got to learn to balance your weight on one toe. Once you have gotten the hang of that, you will be gliding all over the place. You should start by practicing standing on both toes, while holding on to a wall. The more you practice the more comfortable you will feel on your toes. Soon you will be able to stand for a few seconds without holding on. Then you will be ready to start learning the moon walk. You start with both feet together. Lean your right foot forward and position it on the toes. Shift most of your weight to that toe until you can slide the left foot straight back. Next the weight shifts to the left foot, so that the right foot can slide back to meet the left one. Then you just repeat the move over again and you are moonwalking. Remember, at first it will look rough and uncoordinated. But, if you just give it a little time and effort, you'll moonwalk slick and smooth. Glide on!

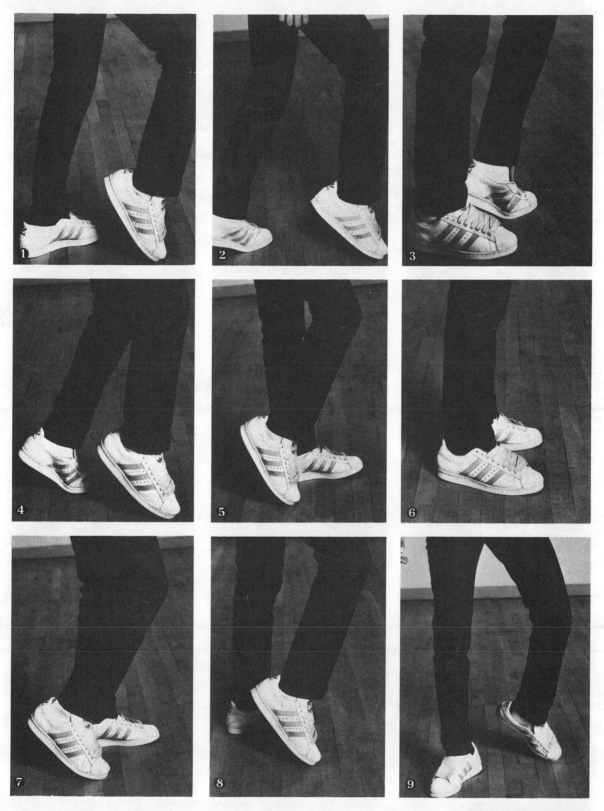

Starbreaking
Break Dancing...Celebrity Style

t he Del Taco fast food restaurant in Hollywood, California, is packed as usual. People jam the place inside, the parking lot is full and the drive-through lane has 10 cars waiting in line, their passengers anxious to pass through and place their orders.

Suddenly a car door slams. Music starts blaring from a shiny black Porsche and a lean, tall figure, clad in shimmery silver pants, windbreaker top and tennis shoes, a hat pulled low over his forehead, steps out of the car and swings himself gracefully onto the roof of the car.

Then, without skipping a beat, he drops down to his back, his legs in the air, and begins whirling in small circles, spinning with elegance, his feet manuevering in the air to keep his momentum going.

"Hey, it's a break dancer!" someone shouts, and soon the cars waiting in line are driverless, all thoughts of food forgotten as a crowd surrounds the car. Hands begin clapping, bodies sway as they cheer the young dancer on.

It isn't until the restaurant manager steps in and signals the cars to move on through the line that the customers reluctantly go back to their cars and the break dancer scrambles into the Porsche, his identity unknown to those who enjoyed his performance.

"That's the way I like it," grins 19-year-old Todd Bridges, who stars on television's hit series, *Diff'rent Strokes*. "In fact, I've kept the fact that I breakdance such a secret in the last year, that even Gary Coleman and my other TV co-stars didn't know I did it until our wrap party at the end of the shooting season a few months ago.

"We were all having such a good time that before I knew it I was on the floor on my back, breakdancing away. Now they want me to show what I can do on one of the show's next season. I guess I will, but then it won't be a secret anymore!"

Why is the young actor so secretive about his talent? "I only dance because I enjoy it," Todd explains. "I really don't want anyone making a fuss about it, and although I do dance in public sometimes—when I go to clubs or if the mood is right, mostly I just do it at home alone or with friends who break, too."

Like a lot of dancers, Todd learned the routines on his own. "In the beginning, I used to go to Westwood—that's a college town in Southern California not far from where I live—and kids would be breaking on the street corners. I just started watching them, then I'd go home and see what I could do."

Todd laughingly says that at first he thought he could pick it up easily without too much effort, but he soon learned how much time was involved. "It takes a lot of practice," he admits. "I really admire and respect those dancers who have perfected their form. When I began spending time at it myself, I realized what they've gone through. It's tough!"

Although Todd is modest about his dancing abilities, his mom, Betty Bridges, isn't. "Todd's a great breaker," she says proudly. "He comes up with his own steps and routines and handles himself just like a pro."

Despite his expertise as a break dancer, Todd says he has no interest in pursuing it further. "I'm happy with what I know now, with what I can do. Oh, it's fun to break when I'm out at a club, or once in a while somewhere where it's least expected, or to pass the time, but I'm not looking to make a name as a dancer."

One actor who already has made a name as a dancer is Billy Hufsey, who stars as "Christopher Donlon" on the internationally popular series, *Fame*. Not unlike the character he portrays, Billy realizes that success is the gift of hard work and dedication, and he's certainly hard working and dedicated.

Although Billy's career encompasses all aspects of entertainment, it's dancing that first interested him, so breaking came very naturally for him. In fact, Billy himself is a street kid. He was born in Brook Park, Ohio and spent his youth in a mixed ethnic neighborhood. The youngest child in a close-knit German/Irish family, Billy gravitated toward the arts to express his inner turmoil and idealism. With the strength of a halfback, he was able to excel in

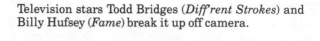

Television stars Todd Bridges (*Diff'rent Strokes*) and Billy Hufsey (*Fame*) break it up off camera.

athletics during high school where he became an undefeated welterweight Golden Glove competitor and was honored as the school's "Outstanding Athlete." In 1979 he became the United States Singles Disco Champion as well, proving that even an athlete can have the grace of a dancer!

Breakdancing may only have become a recognized dance form in the last year, but it's been a part of the street scene for a long time. "That's where I learned it," says Billy. "On the streets. We did it on the pavement if we had to, on cardboard or wood if we were lucky! If we couldn't get down to do it, we stayed upright, doing angular, robot-like movements that included a lot of turns and twists.

While it's true that Billy did study dance when he decided he had an instinctive feel for it, and headed to New York, he never had to practice breaking. "I guess you could say I already was doing it when it was just part of the street scene and hadn't gone Hollywood," he smiles.

His advice to anyone interested in breaking? "Get out on the street and observe what's going on. Watch the moves and the way the dancer gets up and down. Talk to them if you can and maybe get someone to show you the basic moves—then practice!"

One young black dancer who's an expert breaker is *Solid Gold*'s Cooley. Like Billy, he's also a self-taught dancer whose training has come directly from the streets. "When I was younger," he reveals, "dancing kept me from getting involved in bad things, not going to school and that sort of stuff. I spent all my free time dancing on the street corners and at local contests, and I rehearsed my moves in front of curious bystanders most of the time. Breakdancing wasn't a phenomenon like it is now, so I got stared at a lot!"

Cooley says that at first his dancing wasn't taken seriously because it seemed strange to everyone. "Then I started doing the backslide which is a smooth backward glide and I performed it at a talent show. Everybody ran onstage when I was finished to see if there was an escalator under my feet because I had done the step so smoothly."

Of course that backslide gave Cooley the recognition he needed to start his career and a few years later while dancing on *Soul Train*, Michael Jackson saw the move and called Cooley. "I spent a week teaching the move to him," Cooley beams proudly.

"I got into dance because I wanted to make history," exclaims popular street dancer Adolfo Quinones, better known as Shabba-Doo. He got his start as the youngest member of the Lockers, the now-legendary early 1970's Los Angeles dance troupe, and now has a group of young dancers he trains and sponsors. "I help out the younger kids. They shouldn't have to run into a brick wall if I've already been there and know how to help them avoid it," he says in reference to his street dance gang.

And they're popular, too—"You wouldn't believe how many people are always following us around, acting like us, dressing like us, even taking on part of our personalities," Shabba Doo says. "I worked my way up from nothing, just dancing on Hollywood Boulevard. I made up my own moves and then I'd see people try to steal them.

"I'd get furious, but then I met Michael Jackson and he said that if somebody likes the way you're dancing, it should give you a feeling of pride because you must be good if someone is trying to do it."

More and more young entertainers are getting into breaking. Matthew Laborteaux from *The Whiz Kids* got hooked on it "watching kids on the street. It looked like they were having such a good time just getting down and doing it I thought I'd try it, too."

Matt's co-stars on the series, Todd Porter and Jeffrey Jacquet are breakers, too. "I think I first got interested in it when I saw *Flashdance*," 16-year-old Jeffrey says. "Some of the kids I hung around with at school got hooked also, so we decided to learn to-

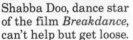
Shabba Doo, dance star of the film *Breakdance*, can't help but get loose.

The cast that breaks together stays together! *Whiz Kids* co-stars Matt Laborteaux, Jeffrey Jackquet and Todd Porter are all down with the breaks. Above: Laborteaux chats with break-dance instructors Sugar Pop and P. Pruett.

gether. I took a couple of lessons to polish my moves—you know, pick up the subtle qualities that make it better, but other than that, you just learn from doing it and you get better and look better doing it the more you do it."

Jeffrey goes on to say that when *The Whiz Kids* film scenes at Cougar High School, there are always kids around breaking. "I bring my radio and they show me some of their moves—things I've never seen before."

It was while practicing one of these moves that Jeffrey injured his thumb. "I break on my fingertips, not flathanded, and I came down on my thumb and it jammed," he sighs, rubbing the injured extremity. Now I can't do hand-spins for a while, and those are my favorite!"

How would he rate himself as a breaker? "Well, I'm not as good as Kid Freeze or SugarPop, they're phenomenal, but I'd say I'm okay. I can hold my ground."

And Jeffrey doesn't find breaking easier than other dance forms. "You've got to keep the beat just like you do in any kind of dancing, and it's tiring. You can only do it for so long before you get exhausted."

Jeffrey and Matthew were able to show off their breaking talents last season on their TV show, and both hope to be able to do more next season. "After all," Matt says, "our show tries to be realistic, true to life, and breakdancing is true to life. Everywhere you go there's someone doing it on the corner!"

Matthew and other young celebrities like "P" Pruit (The Tim Conway Show) and Timmy Gibbs (Father Murphy, The Rousters) are having fun breaking, too. Like Todd Bridges, Timmy watched the dancers in Westwood, went home and started working on it. "Of course it's easier if someone shows you the right moves in the beginning," he admits, "so I went with some friends, including Matthew and 'P' to the Los Angeles Dance Center for a few lessons. We met the famous breaker Sugarpop, who demonstrated

Left: Instructors Sugar Pop and Pruett teach every Saturday morning at the Los Angeles Dance Center. These are two teachers that aren't afraid to get down on the floor and show the class how it is done. Bottom: You'll find Lauri Hendler, from *Gimme A Break*, popping all over the place.

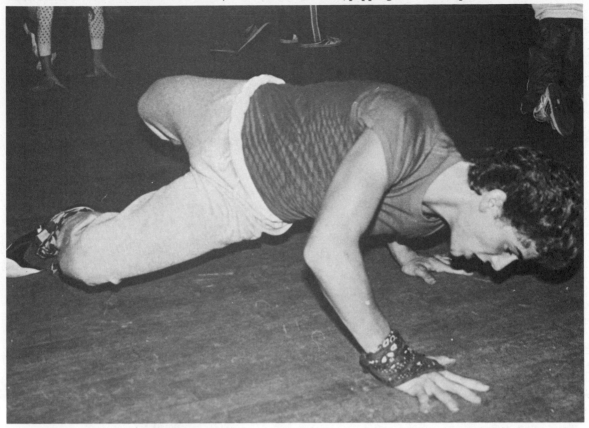

the dance on last year's Emmy Awards Show and is also in Michael Jackson's *Thriller* video, and he taught us. It was really exciting."

"Yes," agrees "P," who's been a dancer all his life. "I was so into it, Sugarpop probably thought I was his third arm I hung around so close!" Apparently some of Sugarpop's talent rubbed off, because "P" got so good so fast, he now teaches classes himself, and helps offer show business friends like Timmy learn the routines.

"I also showed Lauri Hendler *Gimme A Break* some of the moves," says "P." "Not too many girls are into breaking, or they don't seem to be as interested in it as the guys are, but Lauri wanted to learn and she's practicing at it diligently."

Actors and dancers aren't the only ones in entertainment into breaking. Even musicians are using routines as part of their stage acts. Lionel Richie has a breaking segment in his concert tour which features Damita Jo Freeman, an ex-*Soul Train* dancer and professional. Baby Gap and The Gap Band are breaking, and even The Rolling Stones' Mick Jagger can do the moves, and of course, Michael Jackson himself!

THE JACKSON CONNECTION

Mr. Michael Jackson has influenced just about every area of dance. His imposing presence can be felt in discos, dance studios, and even on the Broadway stage. Michael's spirit is pervasive. His music reaches out and touches in dance. While Jackson's music remains outside of the B-Beat experience, Michael is well respected as a dancer. His moon walk is the standard by which all others are judged. In the '70s B-Boys were watching Michael, who had perfected the robot. Today Mike's Robot is the envy of every Electric Boogier.

Michael is a dancer at heart. He loves movement. That is why you saw electric boogiers in Jackson's *Thriller* video. It was somewhat of a thrill in itself, seeing ghouls waving and popping. Jackson knows what is hot and he tries to incorporate these elements into his product. I talked with Michael while he was working on the *Thriller* video. He told me that he was going over the story boards for the video. It was easy to see that he was totally into every area of the production. No detail escaped his consideration.

Michael is an analyst, who dissects and examines every element of dance. I can still remember the look on Michael's face, while we watched a videotape of the *Wizard of Oz*. During a dance sequence, it seemed as if Michael had left the room. His slight frame was seated on the sofa but mentally Michael had joined Dorothy and the Scarecrow on the screen.

Dance and mime fascinate Michael. He especially watches what is new and inventive in dance and mime. With the international interest in breakdancing skyrocketing, I'm certain that it is not escaping Michael's watchful eye. The details of the The Jackson's concert are a closely guarded secret, however don't be surprised if you see some breakers and boogiers on stage with them. Just imagine the fluid Jackson doing waves and back spins on stage. What could thrill audiences more? Certainly nothing that I can think of.

BREAKDANCING 74

Robert Taylor, the 17-year-old star of *Beat Street*, foot works them to death.

BREAKING INTO THE MOVIES

Breakdance has had a major influence on the entire entertainment industry. It was just a matter of time before the film industry opened its doors and welcomed the Breakdancer. Not only have the doors been opened, but the big movie companies have embraced this new dancing phenomenon called "Breaking." There are no less than ten films in some stage of production that have some sort of breakdance theme.

The first examination of breakdance, and the whole B-Boy culture, through film, was a piece called *Wild Style*. This was one of the first attempts to document a segment of the population that revolves around a beat. It was a rather raw and uncluttered look at the music, the art and the dance. The first few films on breakdance were low budget and poorly done. But, that has all changed; Enter Hollywood!

Beat Street was the first sharp, big money production with breakdance. Produced by Harry Belafonte, the multi-million dollar production was the first Hollywood attempt to cash in on the explosive interest in break dance. This production did a great deal of its casting in the streets of New York City. What they have come up with is an interesting mixture of actors that create characters very close to the actual B-Boys. *Beat Street* is a Hollywood view, but it captures the experience of the South Bronx.

The film has gained credibility through the believable performances of some exciting new actors, especially 17-year-old Robert Taylor. This talented youngster may be the best breaker

A new breed of stars is break dancing all over the movie screens. The streets offer a new breed of matinee idols.

you'll find anywhere. The things that this kid can do with his body are astounding. He has been dancing for a long time now and he makes it look easy. Robert lives in the South Bronx and that is also where he was discovered.

Robert answered an open audition call that took place in a high school on his block. He did some moves that really caught the casting people's eye. They took his name and told him that they would call him back, but Robert said that he didn't believe it. Robert recalled, "Then they called me back the next week and I was excited. I had to go to school that day and I had lost the address and the number. I was totally messed up." He continued, "I only knew half of the address and couldn't remember the rest. So, what I could remember I started looking for, but, I couldn't find the place, so I gave up."

Robert had pretty much accepted the fact that he was out of the film. He had no idea that the casting people called his home, trying to reach him. Robert tells how the contact was finally made. "They paid this kid who knows me to go look for me. He found me. I went down to the production office, and ever since then I've been in the movie."

The job of acting is a piece of cake for Robert. He said that he enjoys working in front of the camera. However, he said that it is not all that easy. "The hardest thing is sitting around waiting, because I like to dance," Robert complains. He continues, "I could be doing something better, because I have a lot of energy that is just going to waste. I am energetic, and I want to get up and move." He concludes, "The hardest part for me is sitting and waiting, and they have you waiting for hours. It's unbearable."

Robert knows his character in *Beat Street*, because no one is more street-wise than he. That is why he had some objections to the costumes that he was asked to wear. Robert explains how they were trying to make him change. "When I was on the set they had me dressed the way I wouldn't want to dress. I just told them I ain't going to dress like that. If I have to dress like that, I'll quit and you'll have to find somebody else." Robert goes on, "That's why they fired the director. He had people dressing like bums. I didn't like the idea. He was doing stuff incorrect. They were making us look like the bad guys from the Bronx. You know, bummie, ready to steal somebody's money. We were making a movie, it ain't about all that."

Robert will tell anyone that all he wants to do is practice the trade that he learned in the New York School of Printing; electronic typesetting. However, Bob may have a problem with that. His incredible Breakdancing and his acting may keep him from ever getting into the printing field.

77 BREAKDANCING

AFRIKA BAMBAATAA

Breakers dance to a different drummer. They have their own beat that they follow. The music has to move them in a very special way. If you go down a list of the year's most popular recording's, you probably will not find a tune that is popular with the B-Boys and B-Girls. They have their own musical stars. These recording artists know how to get to the beat and exploit it. Breakers follow and worship these artists with an unexplainable loyalty. The rappers and musicians have been exalted by the beat. However, there is but one High Priest of the Break Beat; Afrika Bambaataa.

Recording for the Tommy Boy label, Afrika is just starting to get the kind of attention he deserves. While the B-Boys buy every record that he releases, Bambaataa has just started to crossover into other markets. With the success of one of his groups, Soul Sonic Force, Afrika is well on his way to becoming a pop star. This possibility might change some artists, but Bam is a loyal follower of the beat.

Bambaataa knows the B-Beat culture very well because he was there in the South Bronx when it developed. In fact, Bam recalls vividly the birth of breakdance. "It started around late 1969 or early 1970. It was a dance called 'The Good Foot', which was based around James Brown's "Get On The Good Foot." Afrika continued, "It was almost like an acrobatic dance. Girls and guys would be waving their hands from side to side. It was a dance of throwing your hand in the air, legs to the side, and jumping on the floor and sometimes coming back up."

Afrika Bambaataa also remembers the birth of rap music and the B-Beat. He said that the South Bronx was filled with D.J.'s. There was one D.J. that started playing B-Beat, or "Hip-Hop," as some people called it. Bam said, "Kool D.J. Herc, was really the first out there with this style of music. He was a West Indian," Afrika continued, "He took what was happening with toasting, like the rapping Jamaicans do on their records, like 'Yellow Man', and he took American records and just played the breaks of records and bass." Bam said that although breakdance started in the South Bronx, this Hip-Hop music came from the West Bronx. Kool D.J. Herc took his D.J. system to the streets, where he rocked block parties in the West Bronx. Bambaataa said that D.J. Herc started the rap. "He would say, 'Rock on my brother to the beat ya'll, you don't stop my mellow," Bam recalled.

Before long there were Hip-Hop D.J.'s all over the Bronx. One of the best D.J.'s to surface at that time was a young man by the name of D.J. Afrika Bambaataa. Bam was pumping the B-Beat

Bambaataa, leader of the Zulu Nation, shocks the house. Directing the careers of Soulsonic Force and Planet Control. When it comes to Hip-Hop, Bam is down by law!

sound to all that would listen. He would rap to this party crowd, "Shock The House," "Shock On" and "Don't Stop That Bodyrock." Bam started to attract a large group of followers. They were a group of young dancers, who were drawn to Bam's Beat. Some of these kids belonged to a gang in the Bronx called the Black Spades. While some gangs were fighting over territory, more and more youths were being drawn together by a new form of music that they could call their own; Hip-Hop, or Bee-Bop. Bam later organized the kids and formed the Zulu Nation. It was a club, or gang if you please, that fought its wars in dance—Breakdance.

The Zulu Nation is still around today. Now, it reaches much further than the South Bronx. Today, you will find members of Bam's Zulu Nation all over the country. You can spot them on the street by the Zulu beads they wear around their necks. Some of the kids have large wood or metal plaques hanging from their necks that read "Zulu." These kids embrace the beat.

Afrika Bambaataa is totally committed to a style of music that he grew up with. As a recording artist and producer, Bam tries to help up-and-coming B-Beat groups to make it. Despite the initial resistance to B-Beat, Bam knows that it is just a matter of time before Bee-Bop tunes are Hip-Hoppin' their way to the top of the pop charts.

STARR KNIGHT

Breakdance has influenced a large portion of our population. The music of the culture just gets into you and breakdance is the only logical response. Peter Knight and Gerald Starr are two youngsters whose lives have been somewhat changed by the Beat. Fourteen-year-old Peter was born, raised, and still lives in the South Bronx. Seventeen-year-old Gerald lives in Boston, but he has spent all of his summers in the South Bronx. These cousins were constantly exposed to the beat and Peter and Gerald were breaking all over the Bronx.

Peter remembers vividly the first time that he saw Gerald break. "He started jumping around like he was bugging out. I thought that he was crazy for trying to do that B-Boy dance." Peter continued, "But Gerald got better at it, and it started to look good. So, before you know it I started breaking myself. Soon all the kids on my block were into it."

Gerald and Peter were always looking for records to break off on. They kept looking for fresh pumping beats. That constant searching gave Gerald the idea that he and Peter could write their own "vicious" tunes. Gerald talked a relative into buying him some recording equipment. At the age of thirteen, Gerald recorded his first Hip-Hop tunes. His cousin added a rap to the rack and thus began the composing and recording team of Starr Knight.

The fellows are presently in the studio, working on some new material that Gerald promises will be on the money. He said that he has a formula for break music that hasn't failed him in the past.

Gerald explained, "The first thing that I do to write a song is come up with a beat. If the beat is wrong, the whole song is trash, and the B-Boys won't even listen to it, not to mention dance to it." Gerald adds, "You know, I started as a scratch D.J., so when it comes to the B-Beat, I'm down by law."

Gerald says that today's break music is almost all computerized synthesizers and that the musicians are being replaced with circuitry. Gerald insists, "The best has to be pronounced and constant. The ideal break tune has about 125 beats per minute. The breaker needs that temp to keep his energy going. It's what keeps him dancing."

Peter, who writes the major portions of the team's lyrics, says that raps can be about anything. He adds, "But most of the time rappers like to brag about them. That's starting to change now. More and more raps are dealing with other more serious subjects. I guess that is good for rap music."

Peter's and Gerald's roots are in Rap and B-Beat music. They

Two of the hottest newcomers to the music scene, Starr Knight. Gerald and Peter are making new waves in the music industry. The youthful pair are fresh out of the pack.

say that they have a love for that sound. However, both of the guys insist that they want to see their music grow into other directions. They don't want to get locked into any one sound. It's rather safe to say these guys won't get locked into anything. They appear to be on the move. Starr Knight is on the rise.

KURTIS BLOW

Kurtis Blow is a name that is bound to come up anytime you talk about Rap. He is another favorite of the B-Boys. Kurtis has the distinction of being the first rap artist to cross over and make a dent in the pop market. His music is still B-Beat, but as a producer he is well aware of the taste of larger mass markets. However, the beat is always there.

Kurtis remembers his early dancing days fondly. Speaking of his first encounter with Breaking, he says, "It was during the days of the house parties. People used to give parties in their houses and guys like me and my gang used to go and crash parties and just dance and steal all of the girls." Kurtis is quick to add, "At that time it wasn't as acrobatic or gymnastic as it is now. They have many more moves now. You know, all we used to do was just do a split and stay down there on the floor and just hump on the floor a little bit. And, maybe we'd go around in a circle and do a little footwork." Kurtis goes on, "Now it has evolved to where they do back spins and head spins."

Kurtis confesses, "We were the kind of dancers who always had to be the center of attraction. We always used to go to parties just for that one thing, to get that crowd around us. So, we would do anything. We'd do crazy spins—we used to spin around four times and just do a split." Kurtis says that's when everyone would say, "Did you see that," and crowd around them.

Kurtis remembers the gangs that used to be all over Manhattan and the Bronx. "At that time there were a lot of gang wars," Kurtis recalls. He continued, "The Puerto Ricans and blacks would fight against each other. There were gangs like the Savage No Mads, Black Spades, and you also had the Peace Makers. I was in the Peace Makers," Kurtis states. "All of these gangs used to fight against each other. These were like the baddest gangs that would ever walk the face of the earth." Kurtis adds, "In those days the gang wars were really serious. It was dangerous back then. We would also breakdance against the other gangs. We used to go to neutral parties and just dance against each other. That would be like a form of gang fighting."

Music seems to be the most important element of the B-Boys

Kurtis sings the music and dances the breaks. Check out the fancy foot-work. He looks like he is having an enjoyable time.

culture. Kurtis offers this explanation. "It's the beat, and the rhythm of the beat. It's like when I make music I think like a B-Boy. I think like a breakdancer, because that is essentially what I am. That's how I got into being a D.J." Kurtis goes on, "I used to love to dance. I'd go to parties and just have crowds of people all around me. Then I started getting into D.J.'ing, because I got a little older. Plus, the D.J. got hot." Kurtis adds, "He started to get into power, so I wanted to be a D.J. So, when I make records I think like that. I think of those old days of my breakdancing and make beats that I would dance to; beats that I would go crazy for!" Kurtis concludes, "That is essentially what rap music is. It is a B-Boy breakdance record."

Blow knows exactly how popular breakdance is. During a recent tour of Europe, he was forced to add some breakers to his show. The audiences all demanded breakdancers, so Kurtis had to hire some. Kurtis has since tried his hand at breakdancing himself. It is taking him some time to get back into the spin of things. However, Kurtis is not doing that badly with the footwork and back spins. But it might be awhile before you see Kurtis Blow do a head-spin or a windmill during one of his concerts.

THE NEW YORK CITY BREAKERS

As with all art, Breakdance has its stars and its superstars. When you talk about crews, one name is bound to come up: The New York City Breakers. They are unquestionably superstars in the art of breakdancing. This group of seven energetic dancers have proven to be a positive force in the field of breaking. They have contributed to lifting breaking from street corner exercise to a professional dance status.

The New York City Breakers became a professional entity in April of 1983. They had been dancing together in the Bronx for five years. It was their manager, director, and choreographer, Michael Holman, that was responsible for the group becoming a viable dance company. And, indeed they are viable. Ranging in age from 16 to 20, the group is constantly working in concert and in clubs throughout the United States and Europe. From New York to Los Angeles and from Rome to Paris, these youngsters have worked with some of the biggest names in the entertainment industry. They have shared stages with the likes of Bob Hope, Ben Vereen, Mikhail Baryshnikov, Carol Burnett, Anthony Quinn, Dorothy Hamill, Brooke Shields, and Harry Belafonte.

The New York City Breakers have proven that their dance is commercially acceptable. The guys are featured in a number of motion pictures and can be seen in Universal Pictures' *16 Can-*

dles. Harry Belafonte's major film, *Beat Street,* also features the New York City Breakers.

The youths have also invaded television. The kids have done the *Dick Clark Show, That's Incredible, P.M. Magazine, Soul Train,* and the *CBS Evening News.* The New York City Breakers captivated a gala audience, that included President Reagan and the first lady, at "The Kennedy Center Honors." It was a salute to the performing arts, that included choreographer Katherine Dunham.

Under the direction of their president, Michael Holman, the group has developed into a well-disciplined entertainment unit. Holman keeps a tight reign on his fellows. His no-nonsense business approach to breakdance has paid off in dollars. Michael is totally involved in the Hip-Hop culture. He had the insight to package a street group that he knew would be hot. Michael says that he would like to see breakdance move closer to athletics, as opposed to art. Maybe in the near future we will see an Olympic event in breakdancing. Until then, we'll just settle for the spins, swipes, windmills and waves of Holman's crew: The New York City Breakers.

THE DANCERS

Breakdance crews are popping up all over the place. Some of the kids are pros and some are amateurs, and there are a lot in between. Left: The New York City Breakers. Right: One of the Incredible Breakers.

Why in the world would anyone want to become a break-dancer? Why would you want to risk personal injury just to do a dance? Well, the answers to that question run the gamut. The risk of being hurt has not stopped many kids from trying their hands at breaking. Kids all over the country are forming breakdancing groups, or crews, to use the correct term. These crews usually consist of breakers as well as some kids that do the electric boogie. One such crew is the Incredible Breakers.

The Incredible Breakers hail from the Bronx. At the core of this group are four talented youths who are driven by the beat. Jose Mercado, 19-years-old, and Anthony Spence, 18-years-old, are the breakers of the group. Jose Diaz, 17 years of age, and Michael Rivera, also 17, specialize in the electric boogie. The guys are kept going by the fiery turntables of D.J. Gabe Vrias, 18-years-old. The group has been performing together for about three years.

Anthony tells how he got into breaking. "I had a lot of friends that used to do it," he said. "I was in the group before and I used to dance freestyle in the crew. And, then it just rubbed off on me, and I just started breaking." Michael adds that he just likes the way it looks. Jose says, "It is a new form of dancing. Something else to do. And plus, it looks good and the girls like it." The entire group agrees and Michael adds, "The girls like it. That is the main reason we dance." Jose explained, "See, if you do that you have

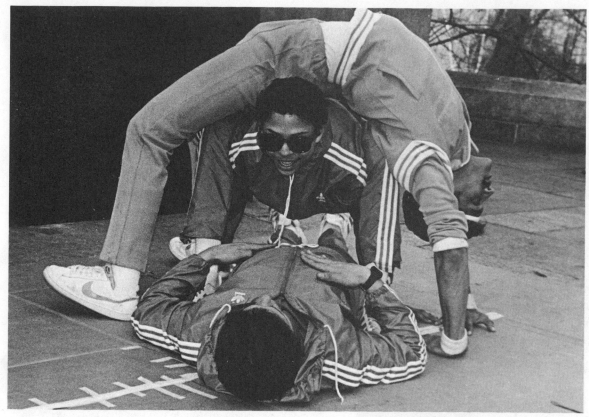

Below: Eddie Rivera congratulates one of his IDRC breakers on a great performance.

like five-digit coordinated numbers (girl's phone numbers)."

There is another group of talented young dancers that hail from East Harlem. These breaking teens call themselves High Voltage. Ranging in age from 14-17, these break and boogie kids rock East Harlem and the Bronx. The group is made up of Adam Torres, Edwin Garcia, Angel Batista, Felix Reyes, and Raul Ratcliffe.

The guys perform professionally all over the New York area. They have a reputation as crowd pleasers. The members explained that there are a lot of crews that battle against each other. They like to have breaking contests to see who is the best. Felix injects, "We don't like battling much, but if it comes down to a battle, we will battle. But, we most like to try to please the crowd. We like doing shows for people." Adam adds, "We're performers. We don't go to other groups and tell them that they're no good. I don't only like doing the dance, I also like watching. You know, it's really fun to watch. We respect all groups."

The kids in High Voltage have fun when they perform, and that comes through to the audience. Breaking is entertainment. It seems that High Voltage entertains themselves as much as they entertain the audience.

BREAKDANCING 84

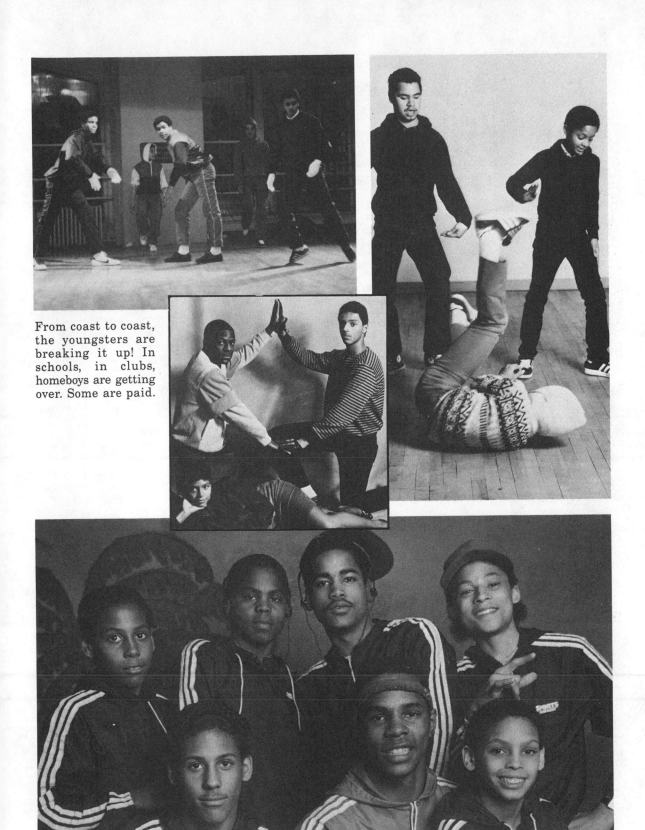

From coast to coast, the youngsters are breaking it up! In schools, in clubs, homeboys are getting over. Some are paid.

CHAPTER

Fashion

Since the beginning of time, every culture that has risen up has brought along its own fashion. Whether togas, mini skirts, buck skins, feather head-dress, or hippie beads, fashion has always been an important part of cultural identity. The Hip-Hop culture is no different. The young B-Boys and B-Girls have their own fashion sense. The kids know what they like and they don't stray very far away from that style. It is like a uniform that they wear with pride.

It is very hard to categorize the kid's style of dressing. It's an unconventional blending of a few pieces of trendy sportswear with athletic gear. The result is sometimes flashy, but always inventive. From head to toe the B-Boy's dress has to be fresh. Shades, sneaker laces, gold chains, and hats, every detail is given special attention.

Seventh Avenue has even gotten into the act. Designers have been working over-time to come up with their interpretations of breakdance fashions. A lot of it is not at all practical for breakers, but they look good. This past season in Paris, a couple of famous designers decided to use breakdancers in their shows.

Despite all of the media hype, real B-Boys and B-Girls will have nothing to do with any of these so-called breakdance fashions. They remain insulated from the suggestions of 7th Ave. Once in a while the kids will select a trendy piece that they like; designer jeans and Cazal frames, an obscure West German eye glass frame. This manufacturer's sales sky-rocketed, because of the interest of Black and Latin youths.

Recently the president of the Cazal company visited a Harlem optometrist on 125th St., just to see the store that was selling so many of his frames.

The basic breakdance uniform consists of a nylon running suit and sneakers. The nylon running suit is used by the breaker, because the fabric offers freedom and a slippery surface for spinning. The running suit is considered wack (un-cool) unless it bares the name of an athletic wear company, like Nike, Puma, Adidas, or Pony. That brings us to the feet, where sneakers must also bare one of the aforementioned brand names. The designer jeans are also worn by the kids, especially the girls.

During the summer, B-Boys love to wear shorts. While many of them are in athletic shorts, more and more of the youngsters are finding their way into the smarter looking polyesters. The favorite color is white. Many even find some fresh short sets. They add their own touch by hanging a towel from the waistband. Warm weather brings out the nylon tee shirts and those tight fitting ban-lon shirts. Now and then we'll see a LaCoste alligator or a Ralph Lauren's polo player on a shirt.

These fashions may seem thrown together, but I assure you that careful consideration is given to the smallest detail. The kids even have a special way they tie their sneaker laces. "Word!"

It all starts with the kicks (sneakers). If the feet are not together nothing else works. This is the only way to lace them. Loosely with no knots, and hide the tips. Also, the brand name is important.

The streets are filled with breakers' fashions. It's colorful, it's animated, it's alive. Kids keep it fresh!

BREAKDANCING 90

Far left: In brass, silver, or gold, the kids spell it out for you. Eye wear? It has to be Cazals, standard, or sporty— fresh out of the pack. Everyone gets to make their own fashion statement. Mix and match, but the look is clean.

91 BREAKDANCING

BREAKDANCING 92

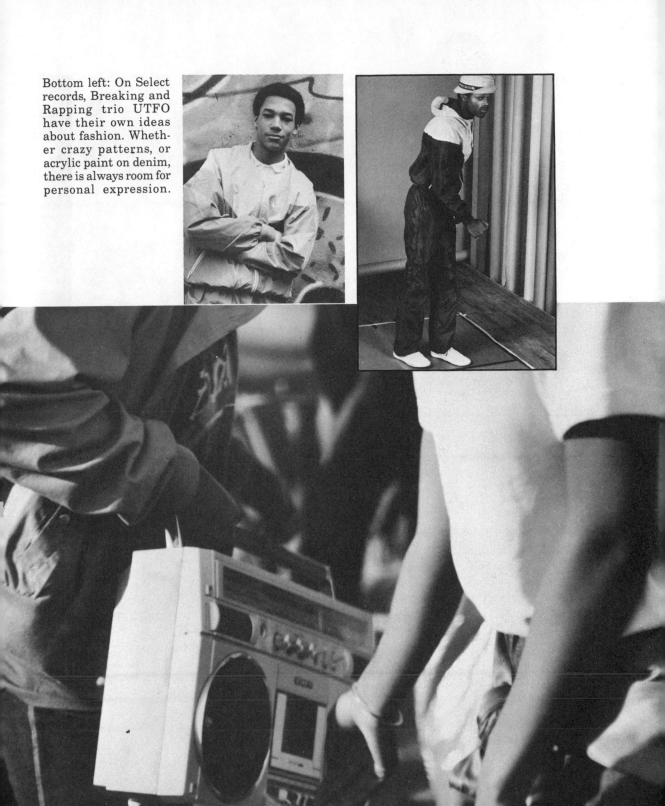

Bottom left: On Select records, Breaking and Rapping trio UTFO have their own ideas about fashion. Whether crazy patterns, or acrylic paint on denim, there is always room for personal expression.

When it comes to break music there is one group that you can depend on to always deliver the beat. These funky rappers are from Queens, New York and the sound is definitely Hip-Hop. The kids in the clubs and in the streets will tell you that the dynamic duo rocks the freshest sounds in the East and West. These talented Profile recording artists are known as "Run DMC." In less than a year the group has come up with its own list of hit classics.

1. It's Like That/Sucker M.C.
2. Hard Times/Jam Master Jay
3. Rock Box

HOT PICKS FROM JAM MASTER JAY'S RECORD CABINET

At the core of the Run DMC sound is an awesome Disc Jockey. His command of the turntables has won him the distinction of being a quick cut mix master. They call him "Jam Master Jay." Jay knows exactly what the B-Boys want and he gives it to them in decibels. He keeps them dancing all night. These are a few of his Hot Picks.

1. CHICAGO GANGSTERS by The Chicago Gangsters
2. SUPER DISCO BREAKS by Various artists
3. STONE by Slave
4. BOB JAMES II by Bob James
5. TALE OF THE TAPE by Billy Squire
6. YOU GOTTA BELIEVE by Love Bug Starski

GRANDMASTER DEE'S CLASSICS

Houdini is one of the most innovative new rap groups around. These young men from Brooklyn rap to the beat of a different drummer. Their music has a heavy European influence. Most of their recording is done in Europe with European musicians. The end result is an interesting blend of rock and Hip-Hop. The jumping D.J.'s who record on the Jive label, are assisted on stage by turntable wizard Grandmaster Dee.

On stage you would see these Hip-Hoppers doing "The Haunted House Of Rock," the group's biggest hit. "Yours For A Night" and "Magic Swan" were two of Houdini's other singles. Keeping the beat throughout these tunes is Master Dee. He cuts and scratches with an unbelievable sense of timing. Look out for Grandmaster Dee, he has a scratch record coming out soon on the Jive label. Meanwhile, here are a few of his picks.

1. APACHE by Arawak all-stars
2. BRA by Cymande
3. DANCE TO THE DRUMMER'S BEAT by Herman Kelley

Two masters of the turntables! Top: Jam Master Jay, who spins for Run DMC. Bottom: Grandmaster Dee, of Houdini.

A special thanks to five of the hottest breakers this side of Fordham Road. Seated, l to r: Adam Torres, Edwin Garcia, and Felix Reyes. Standing: Anthony Spence and Jose Mercado. Ann added thanks to the Bronx for its energy, Manhattan for its style, y El Barrio por la Salsa!

TOMORROW'S CLASSICS

1. RENEGADES OF FUNK by Afrika Bambaataa and Soulsonic Force
2. HEY D.J. by World's Famous Supreme Team
3. SOMEBODY ELSE'S GUY by Jocelyn Brown

GRANDMASTER FLASH

He has to be one of the hottest B-Beat Disc Jockeys around. He cuts, mixes, and scratches records so viciously that people swear that it was done in a studio. Flash was around in the beginning. He was one of the first to start playing what we now call Hip-Hop.

Flash says that the most important element of a good break tune is the drum structure. He adds the majority of the break jams are the product of high-tech. Grandmaster says that fewer and fewer musical instruments are being used. Computers and all kinds of electronic circuitry have taken the place of the musicians.

FROM GRANDMASTER FLASH'S RECORD CABINET

CLASSICS:

1. YELLOW SUNSHINE	By Yellow Sunshine—Gamble Records
2. I CAN'T STOP	By John Davis Monster Orch.—Sam Records
3. SUPER SPORM	By Captain Sky—A.V.I.

TOMORROW'S CLASSICS:

1. DOMANITERIX SLEEPS TONIGHT	By Domaniterix—Street Wise
2. BATTLE OF THE BEAT BOX	By Art Of Noise—Island Records
3. DON'S GROVE	By Donald D.—Electra

Top: Grandmaster Flash left an irate quintet for a solo career. Bottom: Rapping their way to the top is the sexy Us Girls.

95 BREAKDANCING

OTHER STARBOOKS FROM
SHARON

REACH OUT   The Diana Ross story
(ISBN #0-89531-036-8)   Leonard Pitts, Jr.   **$5.95**

PAPA JOE'S BOYS   The Jacksons story
(ISBN #0-89531-037-6)   Leonard Pitts, Jr.   **$5.95**

HOLLYWOOD HUNKS
(ISBN #0-89531-034-1)   Jacquelyn Nicholson   **$5.95**

MUSICMANIA   Robyn Flans
(ISBN #0-89531-038-4)

MR. WONDERFUL   The Stevie Wonder story
(ISBN #0-89531-078-3)   Leonard Pitts, Jr.   **$5.95**

BOB HOPE   Leonard Pitts, Jr.   **$5.95**
(ISBN #0-89531-077-5)

JUDY & LIZA   Jim Southwood   **$5.95**
(ISBN #0-89531-079-1)

THE GLAMOUR GIRLS OF HOLLYWOOD
(ISBN #0-89531-076-7)   Leonard Pitts, Jr.   **$5.95**

THE MAGIC OF MICHAEL JACKSON   **$4.95**
(ISBN #0451-82089-4)

THOSE INCREDIBLE JACKSON BOYS   **$2.95**
(ISBN #089531-086-4)